EXPLORING CIV[

THE RISE

1968

JAY LESLIE

Franklin Watts®
An imprint of Scholastic Inc.

Content Consultant

A special thank you to Ryan M. Jones at the
National Civil Rights Museum for his expert consultation.

Library of Congress Cataloging-in-Publication Data
Names: Leslie, Jay, author.
Title: The rise: 1968 / Jay Leslie.
Other titles: Exploring civil rights.
Description: First edition. | New York : Franklin Watts, an imprint of
    Scholastic, Inc., 2023. | Series: Exploring civil rights | Includes
    bibliographical references and index. | Audience: Ages 10–14. |
    Audience: Grades 7–9. | Summary: "Series continuation. Narrative
    nonfiction, key events of the Civil Rights Movement in the years after
    1965. Photographs throughout"—Provided by publisher.
Identifiers: LCCN 2022039925 (print) | LCCN 2022039926 (ebook) |
    ISBN 9781338837568 (library binding) | ISBN 9781338837575 (paperback) |
    ISBN 9781338837582 (ebk)
Subjects: LCSH: African Americans—Civil rights—History—20th
    century—Juvenile literature. | Civil rights movements—United
    States—History—20th century—Juvenile literature. | Civil rights
    workers—United States—Juvenile literature. | BISAC: JUVENILE
    NONFICTION / Social Topics / Civil & Human Rights | JUVENILE NONFICTION
    / History / General
Classification: LCC E185.615 .L4725 2023 (print) | LCC E185.615 (ebook) |
    DDC 323.1196/073—dc23/eng/20220823
LC record available at https://lccn.loc.gov/2022039925
LC ebook record available at https://lccn.loc.gov/2022039926

10 9 8 7 6 5 4 3 2 1   23 24 25 26 27

Printed in China   62
First edition, 2023

Composition by Kay Petronio

COVER & TITLE PAGE:
Protesters march after
the assassination of
Dr. Martin Luther King, Jr.

Anti-war demonstrators protest the Vietnam War, page 69.

Table of Contents

Congresswoman Shirley Chisholm, page 77.

Demonstrators protest for equal rights in Atlanta, Georgia.

The Way It Was

The year 1865 was an important one in U.S. history. The American Civil War (1861–1865) ended and the Thirteenth **Amendment** to the U.S. Constitution was passed, **abolishing** slavery. This period of time also introduced Black codes in the form of **Jim Crow** laws. These laws restricted where people of color could live and work and were especially strict in the American South.

Jim Crow laws enforced **segregation**. Under the racial policy of "separate but equal," Black Americans could be given access to separate facilities if their quality was equal to that of white facilities. In reality, however, there was no equality. African Americans were forced to attend separate and inadequate schools and live in run-down neighborhoods.

The Fight Begins

As Jim Crow practices continued, two prominent **civil rights** organizations emerged. The National Association of Colored Women's Clubs (NACWC) was founded in 1896 by a group of politically active women, including Harriet Tubman. Members of the association dedicated themselves to fighting for voting rights and for ending racial violence in the form of **lynchings** against African Americans.

The National Association for the Advancement of Colored People (NAACP), founded in 1909, followed in the NACWC's footsteps. The NAACP focused on opposing segregation and Jim Crow policies. Both organizations would be crucial in the coming fight for justice.

Lasting Changes

In the following years, the Great Depression (1929–1939) and World War II (1939–1945) left Black Americans fighting for their lives at home and overseas. The 1954 U.S. Supreme Court decision in the *Brown v. Board of Education of Topeka* case challenging school segregation finally put an end to "separate but equal" in public schools. The years between 1955 and 1965 would serve as the heart of the civil rights movement. Rosa Parks refused to give up her seat on a bus, sparking the Montgomery bus **boycott**. The Reverend Dr. Martin Luther King, Jr., emerged as a leader and organized the March on Washington for Jobs and Freedom, the largest civil rights demonstration at the time.

The 1960s and 1970s further ignited those yearning for equal opportunities under the law. **Activists** continued to persevere, resulting in lasting changes for the African American community.

Thousands of protesters gather at Resurrection City in Washington, DC.

1968

The year 1968 was a year of dramatic change in the United States. In this book, learn how the Memphis Sanitation Workers' Strike united hundreds of African American workers and brought national attention to **economic** injustice. See how the assassination of Dr. King sparked protests across the country and prompted President Lyndon B. Johnson to sign the Civil Rights Act of 1968. Witness the founding of Resurrection City and find out how one hero, Shirley Chisholm, beat the odds to become the first African American congresswoman. And learn how, after 13 years, the costly war in Vietnam reached its height, then slowly started coming to a close. ■

Eartha Kitt was a famous actress, singer, and dancer.

1

A Movement in Memphis

The First Lady of the United States, Lady Bird Johnson, was determined to reduce crime in the country. So, on January 19, 1968, she invited 50 politically active women to the White House for her Women Doers' Luncheon to discuss the issue. Representatives from organizations such as the League of Women Voters and the NACWC accepted the invitation. So did Eartha Kitt.

Eartha Kitt was a famous African American actress, singer, and dancer who'd starred on television, film, and Broadway. She was known for being as outspoken as she was talented.

During the luncheon, Mrs. Johnson asked why American young men were committing crimes at such an alarming rate. Kitt spoke up: The youth were turning to crime because of the Vietnam War.

Anyone with a criminal record couldn't be **drafted**, or forced to join the military. It was better to be sent to jail than to be sent to war.

Eartha Kitt spoke the truth. But Mrs. Johnson, shocked, took this as a personal insult. Her husband, Lyndon B. Johnson, had escalated the war and the draft since becoming president in 1963. Instead of listening to Kitt, Mrs. Johnson unofficially **black-listed** her as an actress. National media smeared her reputation. The Central Intelligence Agency (CIA) started tracking her. Unable to work in the United States, Kitt was forced to move to Europe, where she stayed for 10 years.

Up in Smoke

The Vietnam War was getting deadlier by the day. To meet the demand for soldiers, the United States had to draft young men, forcing them to enroll in the military whether they wanted to or not.

An anti-war demonstrator burns his draft card in protest of the Vietnam War.

Vietnam War

In 1954, Vietnam, in Southeast Asia, split into two separate countries, North Vietnam and South Vietnam. North Vietnam wanted the country to be governed by **communism**, while South Vietnam did not. With support from the Soviet Union, North Vietnam made strides to take over South Vietnam, resulting in war. Fears that communism would spread around the globe led the United States to officially enter the war in 1964. The U.S. role in Vietnam would not end until 1973, and its involvement was considered a failure by many Americans. More than 58,000 U.S. soldiers died in battle, and South Vietnam eventually fell to communist rule. North Vietnam and South Vietnam were united to become the Socialist Republic of Vietnam in 1975.

American soldiers march through Vietnam.

Young American men were chosen at random, sometimes by lottery, to be drafted.

If drafted, a young man would have to leave his job, his family, and his entire life and fight in Vietnam, where 58,156 American soldiers would eventually die.

During the 1964 presidential election, President Johnson had run as the "peace" candidate. He promised that, if elected, he would keep American soldiers out of Vietnam. But within a year, he'd stationed 184,000 troops in South Vietnam. In 1966, his administration drafted 230,991 more men. During the four years that followed, an average of 300,000 young men would be forced into the military per year.

As more and more young men were drafted, more and more young men grew outraged. They didn't want to fight. They didn't want to kill—or be killed. In protest, they began burning their draft cards—small cards containing personal information and a registration number—in public.

In 1965, the U.S. government made burning draft cards illegal. Anti-war demonstrators resisted, stating that by burning draft cards, they were simply exercising their First Amendment right to free speech.

It was up to the Supreme Court to decide. On January 24, 1968, the Supreme Court heard arguments in the case *United States v. O'Brien*. The Court would eventually decide that the U.S. government had the right to make burning draft cards a **federal** crime.

Female protesters burn their husbands' and sons' draft cards to protest the Vietnam War.

The Tet Offensive

On January 31, American support for the Vietnam War plummeted even further when North Vietnamese soldiers launched the Tet Offensive. On Tet, the Vietnamese Lunar New Year, 80,000 North Vietnamese soldiers violated a **cease-fire** and launched a surprise attack on more than 100 cities, government buildings, and military bases in South Vietnam. They even targeted the U.S. Embassy.

Shocked Americans watched the attacks unfold at home in real time on their televisions. More than 500 American troops would be killed in the Tet Offensive.

The Tet Offensive destroyed large parts of Saigon.

A Tragedy in Memphis

The next day, two Americans were tragically killed in their own country. On the afternoon of February 1, rain came pouring down in Memphis, Tennessee. Two Black sanitation workers, Echol Cole and Robert Walker, hurried to escape the rain by taking shelter in the back of the garbage truck. It malfunctioned. Suddenly, the garbage compactor pulled them in and crushed them to death.

Their deaths were horrific. What's more, this was not the first time this had happened in Memphis. In 1964, two other men died the exact same way when their own faulty garbage truck malfunctioned. Yet the pro-segregation mayor, Henry Loeb, ignored workers' repeated pleas for safer standards and equipment.

This was typical—Black workers in Memphis had to endure dangerous working conditions for pay so low that it left them below the poverty line.

Orangeburg Massacre

In 1968, the local bowling alley in Orangeburg, South Carolina, was still segregated. Students at South Carolina State University had asked the owner many times to desegregate it, but he would not. On February 8, 200 students began protesting on campus. Police fired into the crowd, shooting many students in the back as they ran away. Twenty-eight people were injured, and three African American men were killed. The police were cleared of all charges; however, in 1970, the African American activist who helped organize the protests, Cleveland Sellers, was sentenced to seven months in state prison. He would receive a full **pardon** by the governor of South Carolina 25 years later.

The National Guard assembles to stop demonstrators from protesting the Orangeburg Massacre.

Many of them needed food stamps to survive even though they were working full time. When forced to work late, they were never paid overtime. They couldn't afford life insurance to support their families. And they weren't given worker's compensation after accidents. In 1963, 1964, and 1966, the sanitation workers had tried to form a **union** and strike for better working conditions, but the city had not listened.

Segregation Forever

Trouble was brewing all over the South. On February 8, in Alabama, George Wallace announced he would be running for U.S. president. As the governor of Alabama, Wallace, like Henry Loeb, was an outspoken supporter of segregation. His slogan was "Segregation now, segregation tomorrow, segregation forever!"

Even though he and the current president, Lyndon B. Johnson, were both in the Democratic Party, Wallace knew how to bring **conservative** and **blue-collar** voters to his side. He would eventually run as a third-party candidate, not as a Democrat or Republican, and win 10 million votes. ■

Former Alabama governor George Wallace.

Protesters in Memphis announce, "I AM a Man."

2

One Nation, Two Societies

On February 12, 1968, about 1,300 of Memphis's sanitation workers went on strike for safer working conditions, better wages, and justice for Cole and Walker. They proclaimed their slogan proudly: "I AM a Man." They chose this slogan because the mayor, Henry Loeb, often spoke about them as if they were children, even though many workers were in their fifties and sixties. By February 15, 10,000 tons of uncollected trash were piled around the city.

On February 18, the sanitation workers, along with activists T. O. Jones and Jerry Wurf, presented a new list of demands for the city. The new demands included basic workers' rights. On February 22, they hosted a **sit-in** at Memphis City Hall. The City Council voted to let them unionize and raise wages, but Loeb rejected the idea.

On February 23, nonviolent demonstrators marched to city hall in a peaceful protest. The police attacked them with mace and tear gas. The next day, Memphis minister James Lawson, a longtime ally of Dr. King, formed the Community on the Move for Equality (COME) to organize more direct action.

On February 26, the Memphis strikers announced that after they got their immediate demands, they would work toward ending police violence and call for better housing and education for all Black residents of Memphis. This march was bigger than themselves. Soon, local college and high school students marched daily alongside the sanitation workers. Twenty-five percent of the students were white.

The Kerner Commission

On February 29, President Johnson reluctantly released the official report from the Kerner Commission. He had created the Kerner Commission to find out what caused 159 protests during the Long, Hot Summer of '67. Many white Americans called the protests "race riots," and they blamed African Americans for the unrest. However, the Kerner Commission discovered a different cause.

According to the report, the demonstrations were caused by centuries of racial **discrimination**. The police acted violently toward African Americans; this was called police brutality. Unfair legal policies barred African Americans from voting; this was called voter suppression. African Americans received harsher sentences than white Americans for committing the same crimes; this was due to an unfair criminal justice system. Additionally, African Americans were forced into poor housing, received worse public education, and were hired less often and paid lower wages than white Americans.

Even though segregation was legally over, the report warned, "Our nation is moving toward two societies, one black, one white—separate and unequal."

The commission recommended that the government create social programs to fix these inequalities. Instead, Johnson tried to hide the report.

Otto Kerner (left) headed the Kerner Commission.

The Long, Hot Summer of '67

In 1967, between June and August, African Americans carried out 159 forceful demonstrations across the United States, calling for equality. But instead of listening to the protesters, President Johnson and many city mayors commanded police officers and federal troops to attack their own citizens. The largest protests happened in Detroit, Michigan, where 43 people were killed, and in Newark, New Jersey, where 26 people were killed.

National Guardsmen point guns at men in Newark, NJ, during the Long, Hot Summer of '67.

The Poor People's Campaign

President Johnson did not want the results of the Kerner Commission to get out. But they did—in fact, the 708-page report became a bestselling book. The report had a particularly striking influence on Dr. King. On March 4, speaking at Ebenezer Baptist Church in Atlanta, Georgia, his home parish, King praised the Kerner Commission. He also talked about his next cause: the Poor People's Campaign. King had officially announced the campaign in November 1967 with the goal of uniting all Americans around economic justice.

First, King and the Poor People's Campaign would support the sanitation workers striking in Memphis. Next, the campaign would rally protesters to march in Washington, DC, to demand that the government address economic inequality.

Dr. King unveils a poster for the Poor People's Campaign.

More Than Money

On March 18, at Bishop Charles Mason Temple in Memphis, Dr. King spoke to a crowd of between 9,000 and 13,000 people. He declared that the Memphis Sanitation Workers' Strike was not just about money—it was about the power imbalance between Black workers and the white bosses who **exploited** them. Civil rights didn't mean much without economic equality. He asked, what good was it for a Black person to have the right to eat in an **integrated** restaurant if they couldn't afford what was on the menu? Moreover, society needed to begin valuing manual labor jobs often performed by African Americans, such as sanitation work.

Black Power Protest Music

The week of March 1, "We're a Winner" by the Impressions reached the top spot on the Billboard R&B chart. Culturally, this song became an anthem for Black power and Black pride. It was one of the first and only songs encouraging Black Americans to be proud of themselves. The song's message was that no matter how difficult the fight for civil rights became, they had to press on. They wrote it with King in mind. Some of the original lyrics directly named King, but radio stations forced the group to remove the line before they would consider playing it on the air. That year would see the release of another timely Black power anthem, James Brown's "Say It Loud (I'm Black and I'm Proud)."

The Impressions were a popular African American band during the 1960s.

King pledged his full support to the strike. Negotiations with Mayor Loeb had stalled, and local protesters hoped a powerful figure like King could turn the tide. To accomplish this, he and COME would host a march in Memphis on March 22. The flyer advertising the march promised they would use "soul-force which is peaceful, loving, courageous, yet militant." Unfortunately, snowy weather would force them to postpone the march for six days.

Students Strike Back

On March 19, student activists at the historically Black Howard University launched a protest. A small group broke into the university's administration building, where the president's office was, and made a declaration: They would take over the building, and they wouldn't leave until the president addressed their concerns.

The activists stated that the university needed to focus more on its Black students' needs. They

Dr. King speaks to a captive audience at Mason Temple in Memphis.

Students occupy the administration building at Howard University.

requested more classes about Black history and identity. Also, a few weeks earlier, 40 students had gotten into trouble for protesting on campus and were going to be expelled; the activists asked for the 40 students to be allowed to stay. They demanded that the larger student body have a say in the campus judicial system so that cases like that didn't happen again.

Soon word spread around campus that protesters had taken over the administration building. Hundreds of students raced to join them. The occupation lasted for four days. In the end, the school administration met most of their demands.

After this successful demonstration, student activists across the country followed Howard's example. Later that year, Black students at Columbia University would launch a similar protest, and the year after that, the Afro-American Society at Duke University would do the same. ■

Sanitation workers demand better working conditions in Memphis.

3

The View from the Mountaintop

On March 28, 1968, Dr. King held his final march. Leaders of the Southern Christian Leadership Conference (SCLC), a major activist organization, pleaded with him not to go to Memphis; the Poor People's Campaign was launching soon, and they needed him to focus. But King insisted that the Memphis strike was just as important.

King hoped for a peaceful march. Unfortunately, it did not go as planned. It began peacefully, but some marchers started to break the windows of local stores. Almost immediately, police swarmed the scene in riot gear, fingers on triggers.

Minister James Lawson feared that the police would ambush marchers the same way they had on February 23. He advised King to end the march before that happened. King, reluctant but understanding, turned the 6,000 marchers around and led them back the way they came.

It was too late. The police charged. Officers didn't just attack marchers who were breaking windows; they also beat the peaceful protesters, and they shot and killed a teenage boy. Before long, the National Guard arrived with even more weapons. By the end, 300 marchers had been arrested and dozens of protesters had been injured.

King was disheartened. The next day, journalists doubted whether he'd be able to lead the Poor People's Campaign in a peaceful march through Washington, DC, if he couldn't even lead a successful march through Memphis. To salvage the campaign's image, he arranged to return to Tennessee in April for another, more peaceful, demonstration.

King's Goodbye

On April 3, Dr. King arrived in Memphis as planned. At Bishop Charles Mason Temple, King started to speak from his heart, without a script, in what would be one of his most iconic speeches, "I've Been to the Mountaintop."

King discussed how far the civil rights movement had come, from its early days of protesting segregation to its current push for full economic equality. He looked back fondly at the student sit-ins in 1960, the March on Washington in 1963, and the Selma to Montgomery March in 1965.

King compared his situation to that of Moses, a figure in the Bible who led his people, the Israelites, from slavery in Egypt to the "Promised Land." Moses was allowed to look at the Promised Land from a mountaintop, but he died before he could enter it.

Like Moses, King could look ahead to envision a bright future for African Americans, but he knew that he might not live to see it. "I've seen the Promised Land," he said. "I may not get there with you. But I want you to know tonight, that we, as a people, will get to the Promised Land!"

It was his final speech.

When he sat down, he was reported to have tears in his eyes.

Dr. King delivers his final speech, "I've Been to the Mountaintop."

Dr. King strolls along the balcony of the Lorraine Motel.

Assassination of a Leader

The next day, April 4, Dr. King was at the Lorraine Motel in Memphis, waiting for a ride to take him to dinner. Members of the SCLC stood in the parking lot below. King stepped out onto the balcony to speak with them.

Suddenly, a bullet struck him in the head from across the street. King collapsed. His colleagues, including one of his closest friends, the Reverend Ralph Abernathy, rushed to his side. Abernathy cradled King's head and tried to stop the bleeding, but it was too late. King was pronounced dead at the hospital.

That night, in hundreds of cities across America, African Americans led furious demonstrations and protests at the beginning of what became known as the Holy Week Uprising.

Death of Bobby Hutton (Lil Bobby)

On April 6, the police killed activist Bobby Hutton, also known as "Lil Bobby." Hutton had been the first recruited member to join the Black Panthers and was the organization's treasurer. During the Holy Week Uprising in Oakland, California, he and several other Panthers got into a fight with the police. Both sides began shooting. Hutton and Eldridge Cleaver, a prominent member of the Black Panthers, surrendered with their hands up, but the police shot Hutton anyway—12 times. The police were not punished. As the first Panther to die, Hutton became a martyr.

Bobby Hutton was the treasurer for the Black Panthers.

The murderer was James Earl Ray, a criminal who'd escaped from a prison in Missouri the year before. Ray would later be arrested in London and sentenced to 99 years in prison.

Coretta's Silent March

Her husband's tragic death did not stop Coretta Scott King from continuing the work for equality. On April 8, the day before his funeral, she and her children traveled to Memphis to lead the nonviolent march that he had dreamed of, because the best way to honor his legacy was to keep the work going. She also wanted to prove that the civil rights movement was bigger than a single person.

Mrs. King led 19,000 people in a silent march through Memphis from Main Street to city hall.

Crowds gather in Memphis after Dr. King's assassination.

Coretta Scott King

Though occasionally overshadowed by her husband, Mrs. King was a powerhouse activist and author in her own right. After his death, she took over much of Dr. King's civil rights work, became a spokeswoman for the women's movement, and protested for the rights of gay Americans. She founded the King Center for Nonviolent Social Change and succeeded in making Martin Luther King, Jr., Day a federal holiday in 1983. She is often called "the First Lady of the Civil Rights Movement."

Coretta Scott King was an activist and author.

Thousands pay respects to Dr. King at his funeral.

The police and the National Guard stood by, poised to attack. Among the marchers were famous Black figures such as activist Bayard Rustin, musician James Brown, and actor Sidney Poitier.

During the march, Mrs. King said, "I ask the question, how many men must die before we can really have a free and true and peaceful society?"

Funeral of Martin Luther King, Jr.

On April 9, Dr. King's funeral was held in his hometown of Atlanta, Georgia.

It began with a private service at Ebenezer Baptist Church, where he and his father had been pastors. One thousand three hundred people packed into the church. Tens of thousands listened outside, and millions more Americans watched the service on television.

After the service, a mule-drawn wagon carried his casket from the predominantly Black district of Auburn Avenue through downtown Atlanta to the historically Black Morehouse College for a public ceremony. One hundred thousand mourners accompanied the casket along the 4.3-mile walk.

Prominent Black political figures paid their respects. Thurgood Marshall, the first African American Supreme Court justice, attended. So did Carl Stokes of Cleveland, Ohio, and Richard Hatcher

Mourners accompany the casket of Dr. King in Atlanta, Georgia.

Mules pull Dr. King's casket from Ebenezer Baptist Church to Morehouse College.

of Gary, Indiana, who were the first elected African American mayors of large cities. The ruler of Ethiopia, Haile Selassie I, also came to honor King.

President Johnson did not attend the funeral. He did, however, order all federal buildings to fly their flags at half-staff in mourning. Lester Maddox, the pro-segregationist governor of Georgia, refused. Instead, he lined 160 armed state troopers along the State Capitol, ordering them to kill any protesters who came too close.

Holy Week Uprising

For many African Americans, the violent murder of Dr. King, a nonviolent activist, was the last straw. For decades, they had allowed themselves to be beaten, arrested, and even killed during protests, all in the name of peaceful **civil disobedience**. Yet, despite all their sacrifices, their economic situation had hardly improved. And now their leader was dead.

So, during the Holy Week Uprising, thousands of African Americans across the United States rebelled. They took to the streets. They weren't just expressing outrage over King's murder—they were standing up against the racist systems and laws that kept them trapped at the bottom. They were protesting failing schools, segregated and poor housing, police brutality, and job inequality.

Demonstrators protest in Washington, DC, during the Holy Week Uprising.

The Holy Week Uprising spread throughout almost 200 cities. President Johnson ordered the military to mobilize. He attempted to bring the uprising to a halt when he summoned 58,000 troops from the U.S. Army and National Guard and commanded them to stop the protesters at all costs. Over the 10 days leading up to Easter, 3,500 people were injured, 27,000 arrested, and 43 killed.

After the Uprising

The Holy Week Uprising deepened the divide between Black and white Americans. Since the legal end of segregation, white Americans had begun abandoning racially diverse cities. They fled to all-white suburban areas so that they wouldn't have to integrate. High housing prices meant that African Americans often couldn't afford to live in the suburbs, and legal agreements controlled who was allowed to own certain property. Black Americans were banned from purchasing homes. The movement of white people out of cities and into white suburbs became known as "white flight."

The Holy Week Uprising drastically increased white flight. White Americans who could afford to moved immediately. When wealthy white people living in the suburbs no longer paid taxes to the cities, urban areas plunged further into poverty. Without those taxes, many cities could not afford to maintain basic utilities, roads, schools, and social services.

After the Holy Week Uprising, local economies also suffered. Large companies fled, which made jobs scarce. Small mom-and-pop shops damaged during the protests could often not afford to reopen.

Even as the populations of many cities became majority Black, police departments often remained mostly white. ▪

President Johnson (seated) signs the Civil Rights Act of 1968.

4

The Civil Rights Act of 1968

After the assassination of Dr. King and the Holy Week Uprising, President Johnson finally accepted that he had to address economic inequality. Otherwise, the protests would only spread further.

In 1966, King had begun leading marches through Chicago, demanding fairer housing policies in the city. This had ignited a countrywide push for fairer housing and, the same year, civil rights leaders called for Congress to pass a bill called the Fair Housing Act. King had been one of its most outspoken and dedicated supporters.

The escalating Vietnam War only increased the need for this bill. Despite their service and sacrifice overseas, African American soldiers returning to the United States found themselves banned

The 1968 Civil Rights Act also impacted Indigenous American communities.

from purchasing or even renting housing in certain "whites only" areas.

The Fair Housing Act would fix that. Senator Edward Brooke, the first African American elected to the U.S. Senate in the 20th century, vocally supported this bill. He'd struggled to find a home for his own family after returning from World War II. But his support wasn't enough. Between 1966 and 1967, Congress repeatedly considered the bill, but it never reached a majority and therefore never passed.

Now, following the protests, Johnson resurrected the bill and encouraged Congress to pass it within the larger Civil Rights Act of 1968. It passed easily through both the House of Representatives and the Senate, and Johnson signed it into law on April 11.

The Civil Rights Act of 1968

The Civil Rights Act of 1968 had two major parts: the Indian Civil Rights Act and the Fair Housing Act.

The Indian Civil Rights Act protected the rights of Indigenous Americans. It stated that the governments of Indigenous tribes must grant their citizens all the rights and freedoms found in the Bill of Rights. This included freedom of religion, freedom of speech, and equal protection under the law.

The Civil Rights Act made it illegal for banks to discriminate against people based on race.

The Fair Housing Act was Title VIII of the Civil Rights Act. This made it illegal for landlords or financial institutions, such as banks, to refuse to sell, rent, or provide loans to people based on race, religion, or nationality. In 1974, the act would expand to make it illegal to discriminate based on gender. In 1988, it would expand again to make it illegal to discriminate based on disability.

However, not every part of the act was a step in the right direction. Title X was the Anti-Riot Act. The act made it illegal to use telephones, television, telegraphs, radios, or mail to participate in a "riot." This gave the federal government the power to arrest peaceful protesters and accuse them of attempting to start a riot—even if they were planning a nonviolent demonstration. Many pro-segregationist congressmen demanded the Anti-Riot Act as a compromise in order to pass the bill. This was a direct response to the uprisings of the past two years.

Vietnamization

On April 16, the **Pentagon** announced a new strategy in the Vietnam War, which was termed "Vietnamization." The plan was to withdraw American troops from Vietnam and assign their positions to South Vietnamese soldiers instead. This would decrease America's role in the war.

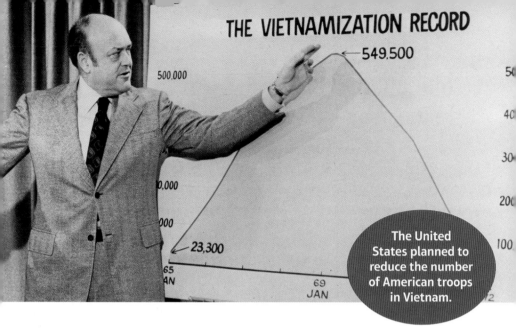

THE VIETNAMIZATION RECORD

549,500

500,000

0,000

000

23,300

65
AN

69
JAN

500

400

300

200

100

The United States planned to reduce the number of American troops in Vietnam.

This did not satisfy anti-war activists, who called for a total end to the war and its attacks on innocent Vietnamese **civilians**. That said, Vietnamization did mean that American troops finally began coming home. Over the next few years, American soldiers would dwindle from a peak of 549,000 in 1969 down to 69,000 in 1972.

A Deal in Memphis

Good news came from Memphis as well. On April 16, negotiators from the Memphis Sanitation Workers' Strike came to an agreement with the Memphis City Council, which promised to recognize their union and to raise their wages. Unfortunately, the council would not follow through on this promise, leading Memphis workers to threaten another strike before the council finally upheld its end of the deal.

Muhammad Ali Speaks Out

On April 27, outside of San Francisco City Hall, a crowd of 12,500 demonstrators gathered in protest against the draft. Championship boxer Muhammad Ali stood to deliver a speech, calling for Black unity and an end to the war. One year ago, he had been stripped of his heavyweight boxing championship titles.

Ali knew firsthand the personal, financial, and professional costs of refusing the draft and publicly opposing the war. Ali, who'd changed his name from Cassius Clay after joining the **Nation of Islam**, was a boxing legend. He'd won a gold medal in the Olympics at age 18 in 1960 and the world heavyweight championship at age 22 in 1964. His nickname was "the Greatest."

However, in 1966, he refused to be drafted into the Vietnam War. Fighting in the war, he explained, was against his religious beliefs as a Muslim. It was also against his personal ethics. How could the United States spend so much money on violence abroad when so many Americans were suffering at home? For refusing the draft, the U.S. government penalized him with a fine, banned him from professionally competing, and arrested him.

Punishment didn't stop Ali. While he appealed

Muhammad Ali displays his championship boxing belt.

his arrest, he was allowed out of jail and continued to publicly speak out against the war.

Committee of 100

After King's assassination, the Reverend Ralph Abernathy became the leader of the Poor People's Campaign. Abernathy officially launched the campaign on April 29. He created the Committee of 100, a lobbying group of a hundred leaders from around the United States, and brought them to Washington, DC.

The Reverend Ralph Abernathy

Ralph Abernathy was Dr. King's closest friend and ally. Together, they had been deeply involved in the Montgomery bus boycott from 1955 to 1956, which desegregated buses in Montgomery, Alabama. They'd also led organizations such as the Southern Christian Leadership Conference and the Congress of Racial Equality (CORE). After King's death, Abernathy became president of the SCLC in addition to the Poor People's Campaign and joined Coretta Scott King in filling many of King's roles.

Reverend Ralph Abernathy worked closely with Dr. King.

There, the committee met with government agencies, including the Department of Justice; the Department of Labor; the Department of Health, Education, and Welfare; and the Department of Housing and Urban Development. By meeting directly with political representatives, they made sure that each politician—as well as every American reading about the campaign in the newspaper—knew exactly which economic reforms they wanted.

The Committee of 100 presented the country's leaders with a $12 billion Economic Bill of Rights, modeled on the Bill of Rights in the U.S. Constitution. The committee declared that every American should have basic economic protections. These protections included a "meaningful" job that paid enough to live on, and the "ability for ordinary people to play a truly significant role in the government."

Abernathy took over leadership of the Poor People's Campaign.

Abernathy (center) and other prominent civil rights leaders pledge to move forward with the campaign.

Other requests included an emergency food program for low-income counties, bargaining rights for farmworkers, and the creation of 2 million jobs. They also tasked the Department of Justice with stopping police brutality against African Americans, as well as Mexican Americans and Indigenous Peoples. The committee criticized the agricultural industry for not providing affordable food. And they called on the government to provide more medical care for the poor.

Congress did not accept the Economic Bill of Rights. So, two weeks later, the Poor People's Campaign continued its plan to march on Washington—and stay there. It was the beginning of Resurrection City. ▪

The Confessions of Nat Turner

On May 8, the popular novel *The Confessions of Nat Turner* received the Pulitzer Prize for Fiction. The book told the true story of Nat Turner, a legendary Black resistance leader. However, the book was written by a white man, William Styron. He portrayed Nat Turner as a fool and Black men as violent monsters, yet he painted the slave owners as good and righteous. Ten Black authors wrote a book criticizing *The Confessions of Nat Turner*, pointing out its **racism** and flaws, and highlighting the need for Black people to be able to tell their own stories.

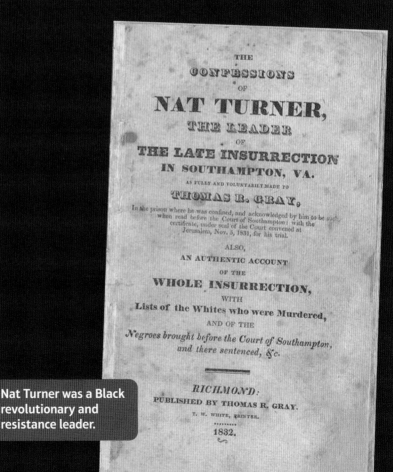

Nat Turner was a Black revolutionary and resistance leader.

Coretta Scott King (center) leads the first march of the Poor People's Campaign.

5

Welcome to Resurrection City

On May 12, Coretta Scott King led the first official march of the Poor People's Campaign in Washington, DC. This march focused on the economic struggles of women. Five thousand women marched alongside Mrs. King during this Mother's Day demonstration, drawing attention to the fact that workers' issues and family issues were closely related.

The march was cosponsored by the National Welfare Rights Organization (NWRO), which was an activist organization for women who received financial aid from the government, also called **welfare**. The NWRO was founded by women on welfare, for women on welfare. They called for government caseworkers to treat them with respect and for welfare aid to be increased. They asked for job-training programs so that they could get decent jobs, and daycare so that they could work those jobs. The NWRO's membership would climb from 10,000 people in 1968 to 22,000 in 1969.

The Trains Arrive

May 12 was also the day that the first Freedom Train arrived.

The "Train" was a caravan of buses carrying 300 activists from Memphis. In Memphis, they'd walked three miles beside mules and wagons to symbolize the unfair agricultural practices, from plantations to sharecropping, that historically trapped Black Americans in servitude. At the end of the three miles, the activists boarded buses to Marks, Mississippi. They chose Marks because it was the poorest town in the poorest county in the poorest state in the country. From Marks, they rode to Washington, DC.

On May 13, another caravan left Marks, but they didn't use buses. They traveled by wagon. Fifteen covered wagons, pulled by mules, carried 100 demonstrators all the way from Mississippi to Washington, DC. The journey took more than four weeks. This was called the "Mule Train."

That month, similar caravans arrived in the capital from all over the country, from

The Mule Train carries protesters from Mississippi to Washington, DC.

Los Angeles on the West Coast to New York on the East—and even from Selma, Alabama, a city that had been key to the voting rights movement. Activists represented a wide range of races and ethnic backgrounds.

Unfortunately, the caravans didn't all arrive smoothly. At one stop in Detroit, mounted police officers clubbed and stomped on demonstrators. And the Federal Bureau of Investigation (FBI) gathered information on the activists riding on every caravan.

Resurrection City Begins

Nevertheless, on May 21, the caravans finished arriving in DC. Planning to stay there for several weeks, the 3,000 protesters quickly developed their own fully functional mini city on the National Mall in front of the Lincoln Memorial. They named their new 16-acre settlement Resurrection City.

Hundreds of activists construct houses at Resurrection City.

It rained nonstop in Resurrection City.

Resurrection City included a dining hall, medical center, and community government buildings such as a city hall. It even had its own zip code. People from around the country donated money, food, clothing, and blankets for the protesters, and doctors and dentists offered their services for free.

Trouble in Resurrection City

Dr. King had envisioned Resurrection City and the Poor People's Campaign as an efficient, coordinated civil disobedience movement. Unfortunately, that never quite came true.

During the day, Resurrection City protesters spent most of their time not in the city, but in government buildings. They met with as many politicians as they could to request economic reform, but the politicians were not always receptive to their ideas.

Hawthorne School

A few miles away from Resurrection City, a group of culturally diverse activists from the Poor People's Campaign took up residence inside a high school called the Hawthorne School. They created a vibrant community where **Chicano** activists, Black demonstrators, and poor white activists from Appalachia could learn about one another's cultures while working together. They organized demonstrations all over Washington, DC, including one to the U.S. Supreme Court on May 29, and eventually earned the nickname "Freedom School."

A pianist performs for the crowd at the Hawthorne School in Washington, DC.

Back in the city itself, members of the FBI pretended to be journalists so that they could sneak around. They paid activists for information, and they wiretapped participants so that they could spy on them.

On top of that, Resurrection City was getting too crowded. It was built to house 3,000 people, but 7,000 had arrived and more came every day. There weren't enough places for them to sleep. Constant rain turned the ground to mud.

To keep participants' morale high, Resurrection City developed an "RC squad" that walked through the camp to lend a hand where needed. Activist Stokely Carmichael, actors Sidney Poitier and Marlon Brando, and the mayor of DC, Walter E. Washington, also visited the protesters. A young reverend named Jesse Jackson gave speeches and sermons. Jackson would later represent DC as a shadow senator—a nonvoting congressional senator—and eventually run for president of the United States.

Reverend Jesse Jackson on May 22, 1968, in Resurrection City.

Assassination of Robert F. Kennedy

On June 5, the Poor People's Campaign—and the country—suffered another setback.

Senator Robert F. Kennedy of New York had just won the California Democratic presidential primary. Brother of President John F. Kennedy, who was assassinated in 1963, Robert was on track to become the Democratic presidential candidate. He was set to face off against Richard Nixon in the upcoming general election.

Kennedy strongly supported civil rights and the Poor People's Campaign; in fact, he'd given Dr. King the idea to bring the campaign to Washington. His wife, Ethel Kennedy, was even involved with demonstrations at Resurrection City. If Kennedy was elected, the campaign might succeed.

On June 5, he was giving a speech to his supporters at the Ambassador Hotel in Los Angeles, California, speaking about bringing the divided country together. Suddenly, a young man named Sirhan shot him several times. Kennedy died the next day.

Senator Robert F. Kennedy was assassinated on June 5, 1968.

Activists from the Poor People's Campaign were devastated. First, they'd lost King. Now they lost one of their few true political allies.

The funeral procession on June 8 passed through Resurrection City.

Solidarity Day

A little more than a week later, Resurrection City held its largest event, Solidarity Day, on June 19. Solidarity Day in Washington, DC, brought together a racially diverse crowd of over 50,000 people. Speakers included Abernathy and Coretta Scott King, who both made statements against the Vietnam War. They were joined by Indigenous American activist Martha Grass, leaders of the SCLC, and even politicians Eugene

REDEEM THE AMERICAN PROMISE LIFE, LIBERTY, HAPPINESS FOR ALL

Protesters from the Poor People's Campaign wade in the reflecting pool at the Lincoln Memorial.

McCarthy and Hubert Humphrey, who were hoping to secure the Democratic nomination after Kennedy's death.

Solidarity Day, or Juneteenth, also called Jubilee Day and Black Independence Day, is a holiday that honors the emancipation of enslaved African Americans.

"Today is really only the beginning," Abernathy told the crowd.

Unfortunately, Abernathy was incorrect. That day was closer to the end, at least for Resurrection City. Organizers of the Poor People's Campaign had been required to get a permit to open Resurrection City, and on June 23, that permit expired. Police violently evicted its inhabitants on June 24, arresting 288 demonstrators, including Abernathy. Officers in riot gear shot tear gas into the crowds. Washington, DC, declared a curfew and a state of emergency, and 450 National Guardsmen were deployed to patrol the city.

In total, Resurrection City had been allowed to exist for 42 days; it rained 29 of those days.

Although the Economic Bill of Rights never passed, the Poor People's Campaign achieved several of its goals. The U.S. government agreed to expand food stamps, supply food to the thousand poorest counties in the country, and provide more funding for public schoolchildren. ■

Jones v. Mayer

On June 17, building on the Civil Rights Act that had been passed a few months earlier, the Supreme Court case *Jones v. Mayer* banned racial discrimination when selling or renting housing. This gave Congress the power to step in and regulate the sale of housing to prevent discrimination.

Joseph Lee Jones (right) and his wife, Barbara Jo Jones.

Charlene Mitchell became the first Black female presidential candidate.

6

The Cost of Black Power

On July 4, 1968, the United States saw the nomination of its first Black female presidential candidate. The Communist Party of America nominated Charlene Mitchell for the upcoming presidential election.

The following month, on August 1, President Johnson signed the most massive fair housing bill in the United States to date: the Housing and Urban Development Act of 1968. Johnson himself considered it one of the 10 most important bills ever passed. He called it "the most farsighted, the most comprehensive, the most massive housing program in all American history." It funded new affordable housing projects at historically high levels.

Going hand in hand with the Fair Housing Act passed three months earlier, the Housing and

Urban Development Act of 1968 promised funds to improve 26 million housing units in the United States within a decade. Six million of those housing units would be for lower-income families.

Additionally, the act helped low-income Americans afford rent. It increased the construction of affordable public housing so that more Americans could purchase homes. And it funded research into building energy-efficient, easy-to-assemble housing that could be developed in large numbers quickly.

Within the first three years alone, Congress would authorize $5.3 billion to fund 1.7 million new housing units.

Unfortunately, President Richard Nixon would kill the bill in 1971.

Democratic National Convention

The Democratic National Convention (DNC) took place in Chicago, Illinois, from August 26 to August 29. Activist organizations from across the country gathered to protest at the convention. This included the anti-war group Women Strike for Peace, the **pacifist** American Friends Service Community, the radical free speech group Youth International Party (Yippies), and the Black Panthers.

Before the convention even began, the National Mobilization Committee to End the War in

Anti-war demonstrators protest the Vietnam War during the Democratic National Convention.

Vietnam (Mobe) began organizing self-defense classes in Chicago's Lincoln Park. They were preparing to defend themselves against the police violence they knew would come.

The Mobe, led by African American civil rights activist James Bevel, strongly opposed the Vietnam War. The Vietnam War was in its 13th year, and the Tet Offensive was proving to more and more Americans that this war was unwinnable. There was no end in sight to the fighting.

On August 25, Chicago mayor Richard J. Daley sent police officers in riot gear to throw tear gas into the crowds at Lincoln Park. Officers beat protesters with clubs.

Protesters used the convention as a platform, calling for the war to end.

This did not stop the protesters. They continued to hold demonstrations during the convention, which included protesting President Johnson on August 27. The Black Panthers attended the protest. In 1964, Johnson had been elected in a landslide victory, promising to bring peace. Now, four years later, he was known for constantly escalating the Vietnam War, and many Americans bitterly resented him.

On August 28, Democratic candidates at the convention attended a debate about how to move forward in Vietnam. During the debate, 15,000 anti-war protesters gathered in close-by Grant Park.

Arthur Ashe

On September 9, Arthur Ashe became the first African American tennis player to win the men's singles championship at the U.S. Open, one of the largest tennis tournaments in the world. To this day, he is still the only African American man who has won singles at Wimbledon, the U.S. Open, and the Australian Open. Bill Clinton awarded him the Presidential Medal of Freedom in 1993.

Arthur Ashe makes history at the 1968 U.S. Open.

Hundreds of police officers began beating them, chasing them, and spraying tear gas. They attacked anyone present, including people who weren't involved in the demonstrations.

After the debate, leaders of the Mobe marched toward the hotel where the Democratic politicians were staying. Police officers ambushed and assaulted protesters right in front of the hotel.

News teams captured the entire event live for a riveted nationwide audience, who couldn't believe their eyes. The news depicted the demonstrators as troublemakers sabotaging the peaceful convention. Public opinion polls showed that Americans watching the attacks unfold on television supported the violent tactics of the police. This damaged the anti-war movement's credibility.

Bobby Seale was arrested for the anti-war protests at the convention.

Protesters on Trial

In total, 650 protesters were injured during the Democratic National Convention. Eight organizers, including Black Panther activist Bobby Seale, would be unfairly charged with inciting a riot. When Seale asked to choose his own lawyer, which was his constitutional right, the judge ordered him to be bound, gagged, and chained to a chair each day he appeared in court.

Seven of the eight were found guilty. But upon appeal, the courts admitted they were innocent and overturned the charges.

Mexico City Olympics

On October 16, during the 1968 Olympic Games in Mexico City, two U.S. athletes made history. Runners Tommie Smith and John Carlos, who won gold and bronze medals in the 200-meter race, each raised a Black power salute and bowed their heads during "The Star-Spangled Banner."

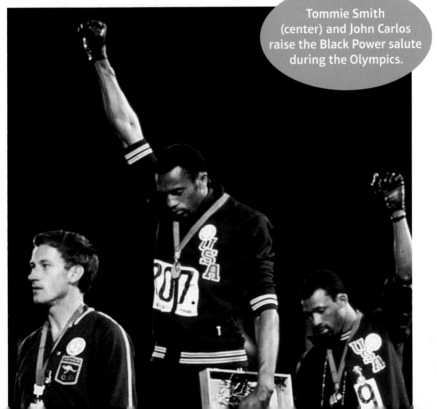

Tommie Smith (center) and John Carlos raise the Black Power salute during the Olympics.

Both men accepted their medals shoeless to represent Black poverty. Smith wore a black scarf to signal Black pride. Carlos's unzipped tracksuit symbolized solidarity with blue-collar workers, and his beaded necklace represented victims of lynching.

Peter Norman, the white Australian athlete who won second place, wore an Olympic Project for Human Rights (OPHR) badge in solidarity. OPHR was an organization dedicated to fighting the exploitation of Black athletes at the Olympic Games. OPHR called for the hiring of more Black coaches; the removal of the racist head of the International Olympic Committee, Avery Brundage; and the reinstatement of Muhammad Ali's championship titles.

The photograph of Smith and Carlos became iconic. But many white Americans were furious. On October 18, Smith and Carlos were banned from the Olympic Games, and Norman was blacklisted for supporting them.

Vietnam Cease-Fire

On October 31, President Johnson announced that on November 1 at 8 a.m., the United States would halt all air, naval, and artillery strikes on North Vietnam. He hoped that stopping the strikes would help him peacefully negotiate an end to the Vietnam War—and fast. Peace talks would begin on November 6. However,

President Johnson announces a cease-fire.

the last time the United States had tried to negotiate peace with a country, which was during the Korean War (1950–1953), the negotiations had taken two years.

This halt officially marked the end of Operation Rolling Thunder, the U.S. Air Force and Navy's three-and-a-half-year bombing campaign against North Vietnam. Airmen had bombed North Vietnam to destroy its transportation systems and stop supplies from reaching South Vietnam.

During the operation, soldiers had also sprayed Agent Orange, a deadly toxin meant to kill plants. Tragically, it also caused cancer and heart disease in people. Agent Orange killed 400,000 civilians

An American military plane drops a bomb on a small village in Vietnam.

and caused 500,000 birth defects and millions of cases of cancer in Vietnam alone. U.S. soldiers who sprayed Agent Orange also suffered side effects.

The United States had hoped that Operation Rolling Thunder, which had begun on March 2, 1965, would pressure the North Vietnamese government to surrender.

But it didn't: The operation was a failure for the Americans. The North Vietnamese built air defense forces and struck down planes easily. They captured thousands of American soldiers as prisoners of war. They created bombproof tunnels that allowed them to move throughout the country unharmed and rebuild any roads, bridges, and buildings that the Americans destroyed. The North Vietnamese government also used the strikes as **propaganda** to discourage Vietnamese citizens from supporting the Americans.

With Johnson's halt, it seemed as if America was finally on the path to peace. However, the next president, Richard M. Nixon, would resume bombing in 1969.

Shirley Chisholm

On November 5, 1968, conservative Republican Richard M. Nixon won the 1968 presidential election.

On the same day, politician Shirley Chisholm won a seat in the United States House of Representatives to become the first Black woman elected to Congress. The daughter of immigrants, she became interested in politics at a young age. Chisholm decided to become a nursery school teacher instead of pursuing a political career, because she would never win enough votes to be elected president.

Congresswoman Shirley Chisholm.

While teaching, Chisholm remained politically active. She participated in political groups such as the NAACP, League of Women Voters, Urban League, and Unity Democratic Club. From 1964 to 1968, she served in the New York State legislature, before being elected to the U.S. House of Representatives in 1968.

Four years later, in 1972, Chisholm ran in the presidential election. She won 152 delegates during the Democratic primaries but ultimately dropped out. She was the first woman and first African American candidate for president from one of the two major parties, Republican and Democratic.

Chisholm served in the House until 1983. During her time in office, she founded the National Women's Political Caucus, an organization for upcoming female politicians. She supported the Equal Rights Amendment, which protected all Americans regardless of their gender. After retiring from the House of Representatives, she became a professor and public speaker.

Turn in Your Draft Card Day

November 14 was national Turn in Your Draft Card Day. Thousands of students on college campuses across the United States attended rallies, hosted protests, and burned their draft cards, even though it was still illegal. ▪

A Kiss to Be Remembered

On November 22, on the television show *Star Trek,* an interracial kiss made headlines. The episode "Plato's Stepchildren" showed a white actor (William Shatner) and a Black actress (Nichelle Nichols) kissing on-screen. This was daring at the time. The network was afraid to air the episode because they feared backlash. To their surprise, both actors received lots of fan mail, paving the way for more interracial romance to be shown openly on television.

Interracial romance was rare on television before "Plato's Stepchildren."

Dr. King's legacy lived on after his assassination.

The Legacy of 1968 in Civil Rights History

The year 1968 was a whirlwind one for the civil rights movement. It was a year of heartbreak and anger. It was a year of victory and change.

Dr. King's assassination left many Americans, especially Black Americans, feeling shattered. The assassination of Robert F. Kennedy only deepened their anger and sadness.

King's death spurred the Holy Week Uprising, a nationwide wave of demonstrations that forced the president to address the country's economic divide. This led to the passage of two housing acts: the Fair Housing Act within the Civil Rights Act of 1968 and the Housing and Urban Development Act of 1968.

King's newest project, the Poor People's Campaign, did not die with him. That year saw a new push for economic equality.

First, the tragic deaths of Echol Cole and Robert Walker launched the Memphis strikes. The strikes sent the message that Black Americans were tired of being forced into low-wage, high-risk jobs. The strikers demanded labor rights, and, after King's death, they won.

Next, Resurrection City took the plight of the poor straight to Washington, DC. A cross-cultural movement of this scale had never been seen before, uniting low-income Americans of different racial and religious backgrounds. Although they didn't succeed in passing the Economic Bill of Rights, they persuaded politicians to support small but notable pieces of economic **legislation** and laid the groundwork for a wider multicultural labor movement.

After years of anti-war protests from organizations such as the Mobe, President Johnson was finally starting to untangle America from Vietnam. Vietnamization promised to bring American troops home. Operation

Thousands of activists moved into Resurrection City.

Rolling Thunder came to a close. The draft, many Americans hoped, would soon end.

At the end of 1968, the civil rights movement and the anti-war movement both stood at a crossroads. The civil rights movement had lost King. Figures like Coretta Scott King and the Reverend Ralph Abernathy were ready to take his place, but could they be as successful? The Vietnam War seemed to be winding down, but it wasn't over yet. How long would Johnson's temporary cease-fire last? The Mobe still had a lot of work to do.

Economic inequality remained an issue. The housing acts were a step in the right direction, but the country still lacked an Economic Bill of Rights that would guarantee the economic well-being of all Americans. Until that passed, Black Americans would remain vulnerable.

Going forward, getting civil rights legislation passed would be more difficult than ever. The new president, Richard M. Nixon, made it clear that he was ready to stop funding Johnson's civil rights bills and undo a decade of activists' hard work.

Activists faced an uphill battle. But they were determined to keep fighting.

The next few years would bring even more change.

Charlene Mitchell

In 1972, when Shirley Chisholm became the first female Black presidential candidate of a major party, she was following in the footsteps of politician Charlene Mitchell. On July 3, 1968, Mitchell became the first Black female candidate to run for president of any political party. She was nominated by the Communist Party USA.

Mitchell was born in 1930 in Cincinnati, Ohio. She moved with her parents to Chicago as a child, where she grew up in public housing. Her parents were both from the South but had come north with hundreds of thousands of other African Americans as part of a

The Communist Party USA nominated Charlene Mitchell for president.

resettlement wave called the Great Migration. They hoped for better economic opportunities and more racial equality in the North. But they didn't always find it.

From her parents, Mitchell learned the importance of being politically active. In 1943, when she was just 13, she joined the American Youth for Democracy, a branch of the Communist Party specifically for younger members. One of her first acts as an organizer was to join a sit-in to protest segregation at the Windsor Theatre, a well-known Chicago venue.

Mitchell officially joined the Communist Party of the United

Mitchell has been involved with politics from a young age.

States of America in 1946 at age 16. Throughout the 1950s and 1960s, she became heavily involved, organizing demonstrations, connecting other activists, and increasing the party's reach and influence outside the United States. She was a close friend of Angela Davis, another prominent female African American activist.

When the Communist Party of the United States of America nominated Mitchell for president in 1968, newspapers across the country reacted with hostility.

"*I'm a person who feels that it's important for the ideas of race, class, and gender to be intersected.*"

—CHARLENE MITCHELL

Mitchell's nomination is officially announced to cheering onlookers.

Publications such as the *New York Times* ridiculed the party for not choosing a "serious" candidate. The press speculated that the Communist Party USA was on its last legs.

Mitchell knew exactly what she was getting into when she accepted the nomination. She never expected to win. She knew that simply running would give her a larger platform to share her political views with the country. She wanted to show Americans new solutions to economic and racial problems, and launching a presidential campaign gave her the national attention she needed to do this.

Mitchell and her running mate, Michael Zagarell, ran a humble campaign out of the Frederick Douglass bookstore in Boston, Massachusetts. During the election, they only appeared on the ballot in two states. Even so, they won 1,075 votes.

To this day, Mitchell remains politically active.

Later in life, Mitchell became active in labor and civil rights movements across the globe, in countries such as Cuba, South Africa, and Namibia. She remains politically active to this day, and currently works with the Committees of Correspondence for Democracy and Socialism.

TIMELINE

The Year in Civil Rights

1968

MARCH 19

Student activists at the historically Black Howard University launch a protest demanding the school increase its focus on students' needs.

JANUARY 19

Eartha Kitt speaks out against the Vietnam War at Lady Bird Johnson's Women Doers' Luncheon.

APRIL 4

Dr. Martin Luther King, Jr., is assassinated at the Lorraine Motel in Memphis, TN.

FEBRUARY 12

Memphis's sanitation workers go on strike for safer working conditions, better wages, and justice for the killing of two men.

I AM A MAN

MAY 8

The popular novel *The Confessions of Nat Turner* receives the Pulitzer Prize for Fiction.

MAY 12

Coretta Scott King leads the first official march of the Poor People's Campaign in Washington, DC.

SEPTEMBER 9

Arthur Ashe becomes the first African American tennis player to win the men's singles championship at the U.S. Open.

JUNE 5

Robert F. Kennedy is assassinated at the Ambassador Hotel in Los Angeles, CA.

JULY 4

Charlene Mitchell is nominated as the first Black female presidential candidate.

OCTOBER 31

President Johnson announces that the U.S. will halt all air, naval, and artillery strikes on North Vietnam the next day.

AUGUST 25

Chicago police officers throw tear gas and beat the Mobe's protesters in Lincoln Park.

NOVEMBER 5

Shirley Chisholm wins a seat in the House of Representatives to become the first Black woman elected to Congress.

GLOSSARY

abolish (uh-BAH-lish) to put an end to something officially

activist (AK-tuh-vist) a person who works to bring about political or social change

amendment (uh-MEND-muhnt) a change that is made to a law or a legal document

blacklist (BLAK-list) a list of persons who are disapproved of or are to be punished or boycotted

blue-collar (BLOO-kah-lur) relating to the class of wage earners whose duties call for the wearing of work clothes or protective clothing

boycott (BOI-kaht) a refusal to buy something or do business with someone as a protest

cease-fire (SEES-fire) a temporary pause during a war, usually to allow peace talks to take place

Chicano (chi-KAH-noh) an American, especially a man or boy, of Mexican descent

civil disobedience (SIV-uhl dis-uh-BEE-dee-uhnce) the refusal to observe certain laws, as a peaceful form of protest

civil rights (SIV-uhl rites) the individual rights that all members of a democratic society have to freedom and equal treatment under the law

civilian (suh-VIL-yuhn) a person who is not a member of the military or police or firefighting force

communism (KAHM-yoo-ni-suhm) a system in which goods are owned in common and are available to all as needed

conservative (kuhn-SUR-vuh-tiv) in one's political views, favoring smaller government and businesses, and being opposed to larger social welfare programs

discrimination (dis-krim-uh-NAY-shuhn) prejudice or unfair behavior to others based on differences in such things as race, gender, or age

draft a system in which young people are required to join the armed forces of a country for a period of service

economic (ek-uh-NAH-mik) of or having to do with the way money, resources, and services are used in a society

exploit (ek-SPLOIT) to treat someone unfairly for your own advantage

federal (FED-ur-uhl) having to do with the national government, as opposed to state or local government

integrate (IN-ti-grate) to make facilities or an organization open to people of all races and ethnic groups

Jim Crow (jim kro) the former practice of segregating Black people in the United States

legislation (lej-is-LAY-shuhn) a law or set of laws that have been proposed or made

lynching (LIN-ching) a sometimes public murder by a group of people, often involving hanging

Nation of Islam (NAY-shun ov iz-LAHM) an African American movement and organization that combines the religion of Islam with Black nationalist ideas

pacifist (PAS-uh-fist) a person who believes very strongly that war and violence are wrong, and who refuses to fight or to enter the armed forces

pardon (PAHR-duhn) to forgive or excuse someone, or to cancel a person's punishment or other consequences

Pentagon (PEN-tuh-gahn) a building with five sides in Arlington, Virginia, that is the headquarters of the U.S. Department of Defense

propaganda (prah-puh-GAN-duh) information that is spread to influence the way people think, to gain supporters, or to damage an opposing group

racism (RAY-si-zuhm) thinking that a particular race is better than others or treating people unfairly or cruelly because of their race

segregation (seg-ruh-GAY-shuhn) the act or practice of keeping people or groups apart

sit-in (SIT-in) a form of protest in which demonstrators occupy a place, refusing to leave until their demands are met

union (YOON-yuhn) an organized group of workers set up to help improve such things as working conditions, wages, and health benefits

welfare (WEL-fair) money or other help given by a government to people who are in need

BIBLIOGRAPHY

Anderson, Susan D. "CAAM | Mothers of Social Change." *Caamuseum.org*, 17 May 2021, caamuseum.org/learn/600state/black-history/mothers-of-social-change. Accessed 13 Aug. 2022.

"Martin Luther King, Jr. Assassination." *HISTORY*, 21 Aug. 2018, www.history.com/topics/black-history/martin-luther-king-jr-assassination.

"Poor People's Campaign." *Poor People's Campaign*, 2018, www.poorpeoplescampaign.org/.

Stanford University. "Memphis Sanitation Workers' Strike." *The Martin Luther King, Jr., Research and Education Institute*, 4 June 2018, kinginstitute.stanford.edu/encyclopedia/memphis-sanitation-workers-strike.

"Start of the Campaign." *National Museum of African American History and Culture*, nmaahc.si.edu/explore/stories/start-campaign. Accessed 13 Aug. 2022.

Mrs. Lyndon B. Johnson (center) and Eartha Kitt (right) at the Women Doers' Luncheon.

INDEX

About the Author

Jay Leslie is a writer who cares about revolution. Her other books include *Who Did It First? 50 Politicians, Activists, and Entrepreneurs Who Revolutionized the World* and *Game, Set, Sisters! The Story of Venus and Serena Williams*. Connect with Jay at www.Jay-Leslie.com.

PHOTO CREDITS